AF269449

SPAIN

R.L. Van

Big Buddy Books
An Imprint of Abdo Publishing
abdobooks.com

abdobooks.com

Published by Abdo Publishing, a division of ABDO, PO Box 398166, Minneapolis, Minnesota 55439.
Copyright © 2023 by Abdo Consulting Group, Inc. International copyrights reserved in all countries. No part of this book may be reproduced in any form without written permission from the publisher. Big Buddy Books™ is a trademark and logo of Abdo Publishing.

Printed in the United States of America, North Mankato, Minnesota
102022
012023

Design: Emily O'Malley, Mighty Media, Inc.
Production: Mighty Media, Inc.
Editor: Jessica Rusick
Cover Photograph: Marina Datsenko/Shutterstock Images
Interior Photographs: Cesar M. Amor/Shutterstock Images, p. 13; Christian Bertrand/Shutterstock Images, p. 26 (right); DFree/Shutterstock Images, p. 21; Everett Collection/Shutterstock Images, pp. 9, 28 (top), 29 (top); GAUTIER Stephane/SAGAPHOTO.COM/Alamy Photo, p. 26 (left); gkrphoto/Shutterstock Images, p. 19; Ivan Soto Cobos/Shutterstock Images, p. 17; Juan Garcia Hinojosa/Shutterstock Images, p. 11; Leonard Zhukovsky/Shutterstock Images, p. 29 (bottom right); LiliGraphie/Shutterstock Images, p. 30 (currency); Loveshop/Shutterstock Images, p. 30 (flag); LucVi/Shutterstock Images, p. 6 (top); lukulo/iStockphoto, pp. 5 (compass), 7 (compass); Macronatura.es/Shutterstock Images, p. 27 (top right); Marina Datsenko/Shutterstock Images, p. 6 (middle); meunierd/Shutterstock Images, p. 28 (bottom); Nicole Kwiatkowski/Shutterstock Images, p. 25; nito/Shutterstock Images, p. 27 (top left); Petr Toman/Shutterstock Images, p. 23; Pyty/Shutterstock Images, p. 5 (map); Robert Biedermann/Shutterstock Images, p. 7 (map); STEFI PANCHESCO/Shutterstock Images, p. 6 (bottom); tony mills/Shutterstock Images, p. 15; trabantos/Shutterstock Images, p. 27 (bottom); Valerie2000/Shutterstock Images, p. 29 (bottom left)
Design Elements: Mighty Media, Inc.
Country population and area figures taken from the CIA World Factbook

Library of Congress Control Number: 2022940522

Publisher's Cataloging-in-Publication Data
Names: Van, R.L., author.
Title: Spain / by R.L. Van
Description: Minneapolis, Minnesota : Abdo Publishing, 2023 | Series: Countries | Includes online resources and index.
Identifiers: ISBN 9781532199738 (lib. bdg.) | ISBN 9781098274931 (ebook)
Subjects: LCSH: Spain--Juvenile literature. | Europe--Juvenile literature. | Spain--History--Juvenile literature. | Geography--Juvenile literature.
Classification: DDC 946--dc23

CONTENTS

PASSPORT TO SPAIN

Spain is a country in southwestern Europe. It is on the Iberian **Peninsula**. More than 47 million people live there.

SAY IT

Castilian
kuh-STILL-ee-uhn

DID YOU KNOW?

Castilian Spanish is Spain's official language. Some regions have other official languages as well.

WHERE IS SPAIN?
N
W
E
S
Atlantic Ocean
France
Portugal
Andorra
SPAIN
Mediterranean Sea
Morocco

IMPORTANT CITIES

Madrid is Spain's **capital** and largest **metropolitan area**. It is a center of history and education.

Barcelona is Spain's second-largest metropolitan area. It is a port known for its architecture.

Valencia is Spain's third-largest metropolitan area. It is known for its history and food.

DID YOU KNOW?

Madrid is on a **plateau**. It is one of the highest **capital** cities in Europe.

SAY IT

Madrid
muh-DRID

Barcelona
bahr-suh-LOH-nuh

Valencia
vuh-LEHN-see-uh

SPAIN IN HISTORY

People have lived in Spain for thousands of years. Romans, **Visigoths**, and **Muslim** rulers have controlled the land. Christians ruled most of Spain by about 1250.

In the 1400s, Spanish explorers sailed to faraway places. Spain claimed land around the world.

Hernán Cortés took over parts of
Mexico for Spain in the 1500s.

9

In the 1500s, the Spanish **Empire** was strong. But in the 1600s, the country began to struggle. It was weakened by many wars. The Spanish Civil War took place from 1936 to 1939. When it ended, Francisco Franco became the country's **dictator**. In 1978, Spain became a democracy.

Adolfo Suárez González was Spain's first democratically elected prime minister after Francisco Franco's rule.

AN IMPORTANT SYMBOL

Spain's flag is red and yellow. It has a coat of arms. This stands for Spain's historic kingdoms.

Spain is a **parliamentary constitutional monarchy**. Parliament makes laws. The king or queen is head of state. The prime minister is head of government.

Spain adopted its flag in 1981.

ACROSS THE LAND

● ● ● ● ● ● ● ● ● ● ● ● ● ● ●

Spain has coasts, forests, rivers, plains, beaches, and islands. It is home to the Pyrenees and Sierra Nevada mountain ranges.

Iberian wolves, Iberian lynx, wild boars, brown bears, deer, and eagles live in Spain. Grasses, scrub, and many types of trees grow there.

The Iberian lynx is the world's most endangered cat.

EARNING A LIVING

Factory workers in Spain make cars, medicines, and food products. Most people have service jobs, such as teaching or banking.

Spain's **natural resources** include coal, copper, and fish. Farmers grow grains, grapes, olives, and tomatoes. They also raise pigs.

Most of Spain's olives are grown in the Andalusia region.

DID YOU KNOW?

Spain is the world's largest producer of olives.

LIFE IN SPAIN

In Spain, people often eat dinner late at night. Popular Spanish foods include seafood, meats, lentils, and chickpeas. People drink coffee, hot chocolate, wine, and beer.

Soccer, tennis, and cycling are popular sports in Spain. Most Spanish people belong to the Roman Catholic Church.

Paella is a well-known Spanish rice dish. It often includes seafood.

FAMOUS FACES

Antonio Banderas was born in Málaga, Spain. He began acting in Spanish movies in 1982. In 1992, he began acting in Hollywood films. Banderas is known for playing Zorro in *The Mask of Zorro*. He also voiced Puss in Boots in the *Shrek* and *Puss in Boots* movies.

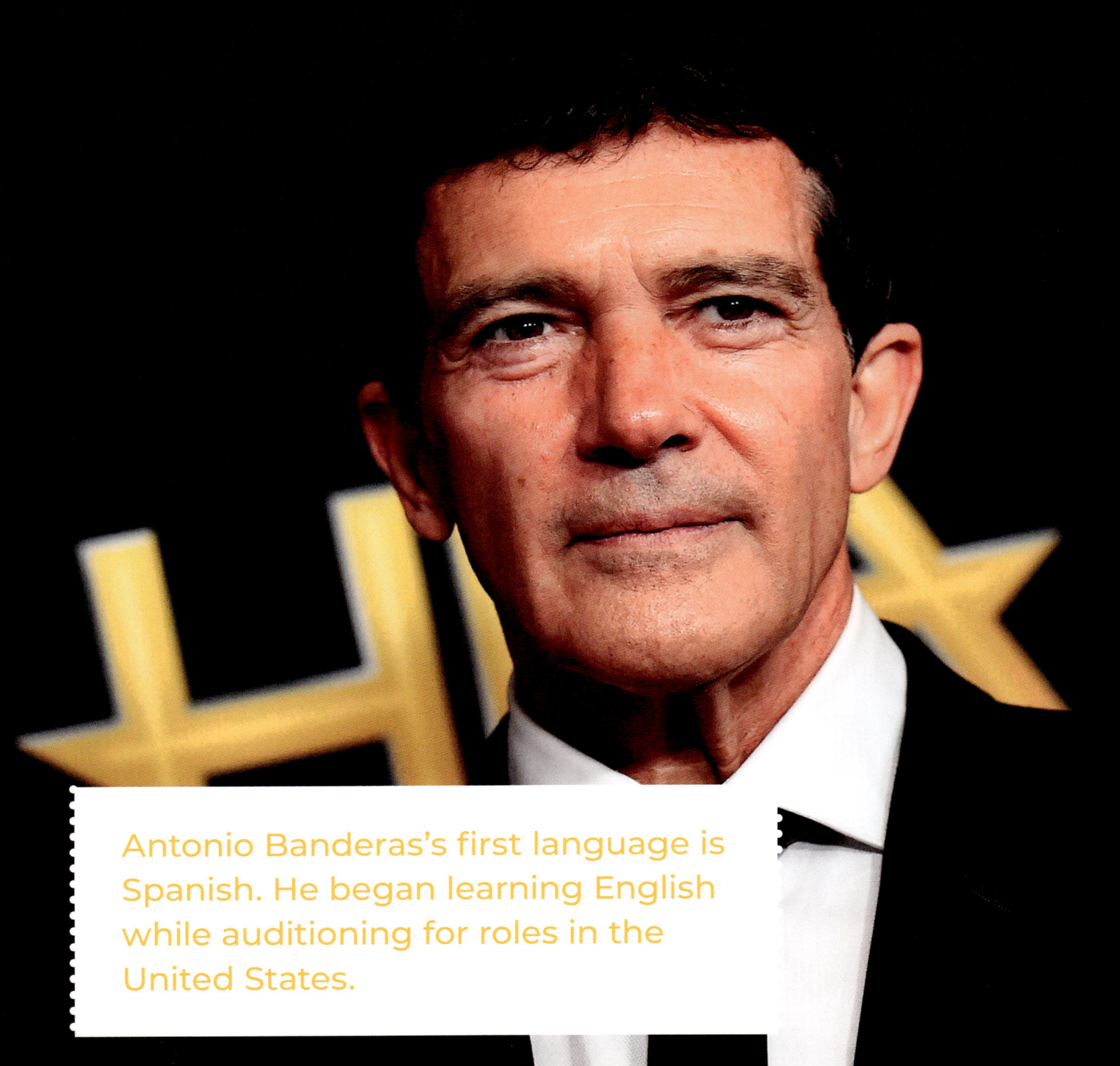

Antonio Banderas's first language is Spanish. He began learning English while auditioning for roles in the United States.

Rafael Nadal was born in Manacor, Spain, on the island of Mallorca. When he was four years old, he began playing tennis. At age 15, he began playing tennis professionally. Nadal holds many tennis records and titles. He has won more men's singles titles than any other player!

Rafael Nadal won gold
medals at the 2008 and
2016 Summer Olympics.

A GREAT COUNTRY

Spain has beautiful land and a rich history and culture. The people and places of Spain help make the world a more interesting place.

Spain has roughly 5,000 miles (8,045 km) of coastline and more than 3,000 beaches.

TOUR BOOK

If you ever visit Spain, here are some places to go and things to do!

DANCE

Visit the Museo del Baile Flamenco to see a flamenco music and dance show.

CHEER

Watch Spanish soccer team FC Barcelona play at their home stadium!

Try some tapas, or Spanish snacks. Favorites include Spanish omelets, olives, and ham.

Take in Alhambra, an ancient **Islamic** palace in Granada.

See works of art at the Museo del Prado in Madrid.

TIMELINE

416

Visigoths began invading Spain. They eventually took control from the Roman **Empire**. **Muslim** rulers would take over in 711.

1492

Queen Isabella I and King Ferdinand II sent Christopher Columbus to the Americas to claim land for Spain.

AROUND 1043

Famous war hero Rodrigo Díaz de Vivar, known as "El Cid," was born.

1519

Hernán Cortés began taking over Mexico for Spain. Spanish rule lasted 300 years in Mexico.

2008

Spain entered a major economic crisis. It lasted for many years.

1882

Construction began on the Sagrada Família church. It is still under construction.

2018

Javier Fernández became the first Spanish figure skater to win an Olympic medal.

SPAIN
UP CLOSE

Official Name
Reino de España
(Kingdom of Spain)

Flag

Population
47,163,418 (2022 est.)
31st-most-populated country

Total Area
195,124 square miles
(505,370 sq km)
52nd-largest country

Official Language
Castilian Spanish

Capital
Madrid

Currency
Euro

National Anthem
"Marcha Real"
("The Royal March")

Form of Government
Parliamentary
constitutional
monarchy

GLOSSARY

capital—a city where government leaders meet.

dictator—a ruler with complete control who often governs in a cruel way.

empire—a large group of states or countries under one ruler called an emperor or empress.

Islamic—something related to Islam.

metropolitan area—a large city and its surrounding cities and suburbs.

Muslim—a person who practices Islam. Islam is a religion based on a belief in Allah as God and Muhammad as his prophet.

natural resources—useful and valuable supplies from nature.

parliamentary constitutional monarchy—a form of government in which a parliament makes the laws. The king or queen has only those powers given by a country's laws and constitution.

peninsula—a stretch of land coming out from a mainland and almost entirely surrounded by water.

plateau—a raised flat area of land.

Visigoths—a group of Germanic people that took over much of the Roman Empire in Europe and established the Visigothic Kingdom.

ONLINE RESOURCES

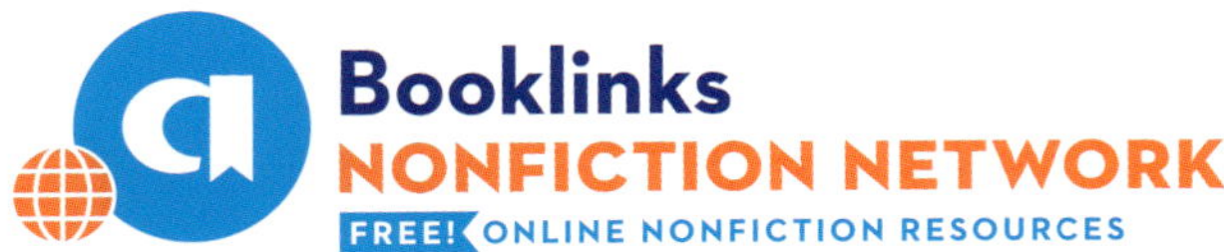

To learn more about Spain, please visit **abdobooklinks.com** or scan this QR code. These links are routinely monitored and updated to provide the most current information available.

INDEX